Mastering Flask in 5 Days;

From Zero to Deployment

Building Your First Web App: A Hands-On Approach

First Edition

MARK JOHN P. LADO, MIT

i

ISBN: 9798307723036

Imprint: Independently published

DEDICATION

This book is dedicated to the curious minds eager to unlock the power of Flask. In just five days, we'll embark on an exciting journey, starting from the very foundations of this versatile framework and culminating in the deployment of your very own web application.

This book is for those who believe in the transformative power of learning and the joy of building something remarkable. May this guide inspire you to explore the fascinating world of web development and empower you to create innovative and impactful applications with Flask.

ACKNOWLEDGMENTS

This book would not have been possible without the support and guidance of many individuals. I am deeply grateful to my mentors, colleagues, family, and friends for their invaluable encouragement and feedback.

I would also like to express my sincere gratitude to the vibrant Flask community, whose contributions and open-source spirit have made this framework a powerful and accessible tool for developers worldwide.

Finally, I extend my heartfelt thanks to all the readers who embark on this learning journey. Your enthusiasm and dedication inspire me to continually improve and share my knowledge.

TABLE OF CONTENTS

This page is intentionally left blank

CHAPTER 1.

FLASK FUNDAMENTALS

1.1 INTRODUCTION TO FLASK

Flask is a lightweight Python web framework known for its simplicity and flexibility.

- **Lightweight:** Flask provides the essential building blocks for web applications without imposing strict rules or conventions. This minimalism allows developers to customize their applications to specific needs, making it ideal for a wide range of projects, from small prototypes to complex web services.

- **Microframework:** Unlike full-stack frameworks that bundle many features (e.g., ORM, database abstraction), Flask focuses on core web development functionalities. This modular approach enables developers to choose and integrate only the necessary components, leading to leaner and more efficient applications.

- **WSGI (Web Server Gateway Interface):** Flask adheres to the WSGI standard, ensuring compatibility with various WSGI-compliant web servers (e.g., Gunicorn, uWSGI). This portability allows for flexible deployment options and integration with different hosting environments.

1

Core Concepts:

- **Routes:** Routes define the URLs that trigger specific functions within the application. They map incoming HTTP requests to the corresponding Python functions (views) that handle those requests.

- **Views:** Views are Python functions that handle incoming requests. They receive data from the request object, process it (e.g., database queries, data manipulation), and generate a response (e.g., render a template, return JSON data).

- **Templates:** Templates are files that contain the HTML structure of web pages, often combined with dynamic content generated by the application. Flask uses the Jinja2 templating engine, which provides powerful features like variables, loops, and conditional statements.

- **Request Object:** The request object provides information about the incoming HTTP request, such as the URL, HTTP method (GET, POST, etc.), headers, and data submitted by the user.

- **Response Object:** The response object is used to create HTTP responses, including status codes, headers, and the body of the response (e.g., HTML content, JSON data).

Benefits of using Flask:

- **Flexibility:** As a microframework, Flask offers maximum flexibility. Developers have complete control over the application's architecture and can choose the tools and libraries that best suit their project's requirements.

- **Extensibility:** Flask's modular design makes it easy to extend its functionality with extensions. Numerous extensions are available for common tasks like database integration (SQLAlchemy), user authentication (Flask-Login), form handling (Flask-WTF), and more.

- **Large Community:** Flask has a large and active community of developers. This provides access to extensive documentation, tutorials, and readily available solutions to common problems.

Addressing Potential Questions:

- **"Why choose Flask over other frameworks like Django?"**
  - While Django is a powerful framework for larger, more complex applications, Flask is a better choice for smaller projects, prototypes, or when you need more granular control over the application's structure. Flask's lightweight nature makes it easier to learn and use for beginners.

- **"How does Flask compare to microframeworks like Bottle or Falcon?"**
  - Flask offers a good balance between simplicity and features. Bottle is even more minimalistic, while Falcon emphasizes performance and is well-suited for

high-traffic APIs. The choice depends on the specific project requirements and the developer's preferences.

Citations (can be added as needed):

- Flask Documentation: https://flask.palletsprojects.com/
- Jinja2 Documentation: https://jinja.palletsprojects.com/ [1]
- WSGI Specification: https://peps.python.org/pep-0333/

By understanding these fundamental concepts, you'll be well-equipped to embark on your Flask development journey. In the following chapters, we'll delve deeper into setting up the development environment, creating basic Flask applications, and exploring more advanced features.

1.2 SETTING UP THE DEVELOPMENT ENVIRONMENT

Before diving into Flask development, it's crucial to establish a robust and isolated development environment. This section outlines the essential steps:

- **Installing Python and pip:**
  - Python is the foundation for Flask development. Download the latest stable release from the official Python website (https://www.python.org/). During installation, ensure to check the box to add Python to your system's PATH.
  - pip is the package installer for Python. It's usually included with modern Python installations. Verify its installation by opening your terminal or command prompt and running pip --version. If not installed, refer to the official Python documentation for installation instructions.

- **Creating a Virtual Environment (using venv)**
  - **Importance:** Virtual environments are highly recommended for Python projects. They create isolated environments for each project, ensuring that dependencies for different projects don't conflict. This promotes better organization, reduces potential errors, and simplifies project sharing and collaboration.

- **Creating a Virtual Environment:**
    1. **Navigate** to your project's directory using the command line.
    2. **Create a virtual environment** using the following command:

    ```
    python3 -m venv <your_env_name>
    ```

    (Replace <your_env_name> with a descriptive name for your environment, e.g., my_flask_app)

- **Activating the Virtual Environment:**
    1. **On macOS/Linux:**

    ```
    source <your_env_name>/bin/activate
    ```

    2. **On Windows:**

    ```
    <your_env_name>\Scripts\activate
    ```

    3. Once activated, the command prompt will typically display the name of the active environment in parentheses.

- **Installing Flask:**
    - With the virtual environment activated, install Flask using pip:

    ```
    pip install Flask
    ```

- This command will download and install the Flask package and its dependencies within the current virtual environment.

Addressing Potential Questions:

- **"Why are virtual environments so important?"**
  - As mentioned earlier, virtual environments provide several key benefits:
    - **Dependency Isolation:** Prevent conflicts between project dependencies.
    - **Reproducibility:** Easily recreate the exact environment used for development, testing, and deployment.
    - **Simplified Collaboration:** Share projects more easily by providing clear instructions for setting up the environment.
    - **System Integrity:** Avoid unintended modifications to your system-wide Python installation.
- **"Are there alternative ways to manage dependencies?"**
  - While pip is the standard package manager, tools like poetry and pipenv offer more advanced features for dependency management, such as creating lock files to ensure reproducible environments.

- **"What if I encounter installation issues?"**

  - o If you encounter any issues during installation, double-check your internet connection, ensure you have the necessary permissions, and refer to the official Python and pip documentation for troubleshooting.

By following these steps, you'll have a well-structured development environment ready for your Flask projects. In the next section, we'll explore how to create your first simple Flask application.

Note: This explanation provides a basic overview. For more in-depth information and advanced usage of virtual environments, refer to the official [1] Python documentation:
https://docs.python.org/3/library/venv.html

This comprehensive guide should provide a strong foundation for Computer Science students and educators. Remember to adapt the level of detail and complexity based on the specific learning objectives.

1.3 BASIC FLASK APPLICATION

Let's begin by creating a simple "Hello, World!" application to grasp the fundamental structure and execution of a Flask application.

1. Creating a Simple "Hello, World!" Application

1. **Create a new Python file:** In your project directory (where you activated your virtual environment), create a new Python file named app.py.
2. **Import the Flask class:**

```
from flask import Flask
```

3. **Create a Flask app instance:**

```
app = Flask(__name__)
```

   o __name__ is a special variable that represents the name of the current module.
4. **Define a route and view function:**

```
@app.route('/')
def hello_world():
    return 'Hello, World!'
```

   o The @app.route('/') decorator defines the root URL ('/') for this application.
   o The hello_world() function is the view function that will be executed when a user visits the root URL. This function simply returns the string 'Hello, World!'.

2. Understanding the Structure of a Flask Application

- **app.py (or main.py)** is typically the main file of a Flask application. It's where you create the Flask app instance, define routes, and handle application logic.
- **Modular Approach:** For larger applications, it's common to organize code into separate modules (e.g., views.py, models.py, utils.py) for better readability and maintainability.
- **Blueprint System:** Flask provides a blueprint system for organizing large applications into smaller, more manageable components. Blueprints can have their own routes, templates, and static files.

3. Running the Development Server

1. **Activate your virtual environment** (if not already activated).
2. **Run the Flask development server:**

```
flask run
```

- By default, the development server runs on http://127.0.0.1:5000/.

3. **Open your web browser** and visit http://127.0.0.1:5000/. You should see the message "Hello, World!" displayed in your browser.

Addressing Potential Questions:

- **"What is the purpose of __name__?"**
  - ○ __name__ is a built-in variable in Python. It's set to the name of the current module. In the case of the main file (e.g., app.py), __name__ is usually set to "__main__". Using __name__ in Flask(__name__) allows Flask to automatically detect the location of templates, static files, and other resources within your application.
- **"Can I customize the development server?"**
  - ○ Yes, you can customize the development server using the flask run command-line options:
    - ▪ --host: Specify the hostname (e.g., 0.0.0.0 to make the server accessible from other devices on the network).
    - ▪ --port: Specify the port number (e.g., 5001).
    - ▪ --debug: Enable debug mode, which provides more detailed error messages and helpful features for development.
- **"What are the next steps after creating the 'Hello, World!' application?"**
  - ○ Start exploring more advanced features of Flask, such as:
    - ▪ **Routing:** Define more complex URLs with URL parameters.

- **Views:** Create more sophisticated view functions to handle user interactions and data processing.
- **Templates:** Use Jinja2 to create dynamic HTML templates.

This "Hello, World!" example provides a foundational understanding of how to create and run a basic Flask application. In the subsequent chapters, we'll delve deeper into these core concepts and explore more intricate aspects of Flask development.

This explanation aims to be comprehensive and informative for Computer Science students and educators. Feel free to adapt the level of detail and complexity based on the specific learning objectives.

1.4 ROUTING AND VIEWS

Routing is the core mechanism in Flask that maps incoming HTTP requests to the appropriate Python functions (views) that handle those requests.

1. Defining Routes with the @app.route() Decorator

- **Basic Routing:**

from flask import Flask

app = Flask(**name**)

@app.route('/') def index(): return 'This is the home page'

@app.route('/about') def about(): return 'This is the about page'

* The `@app.route('/')` decorator defines the root URL ('/') for the `index()` function.
* Similarly, `@app.route('/about')` defines the '/about' URL for the `about()` function.

* **Multiple Routes for a Single View Function:**

```python
@app.route('/')
@app.route('/home')
def home():
    return 'This is the home page'
```

- This allows the same view function to be accessed through multiple URLs.

2. Creating Dynamic Routes with URL Parameters

- **Variable Rules:**

```
@app.route('/user/<username>')
def show_user(username):
  return f'User: {username}'
```

  - o <username> is a variable rule that captures the username from the URL.
  - o The captured value is passed as an argument to the show_user() function.
- **Data Type Conversion:**

```
@app.route('/post/<int:post_id>')
def show_post(post_id):
  return f'Post ID: {post_id}'
```

  - o int:post_id converts the captured value to an integer before passing it to the view function.
  - o Other data types like float, path (for capturing segments with slashes), and uuid are also supported.

3. Handling HTTP Methods (GET, POST, PUT, DELETE)

- **Specifying HTTP Methods:**

```
@app.route('/login', methods=['GET', 'POST'])
def login():
    if request.method == 'GET':
        return render_template('login.html')
    elif request.method == 'POST':
        # Process login form data
        return 'Login successful!'
```

  - o The methods argument in the @app.route() decorator specifies the HTTP methods that the view function should handle.

- **Using Built-in HTTP Methods:**
  - o Flask provides convenience methods for common HTTP methods:
    - @app.get('/path'): For GET requests.
    - @app.post('/path'): For POST requests.
    - @app.put('/path'): For PUT requests.
    - @app.delete('/path'): For DELETE requests.

Real-World Scenarios:

- **E-commerce Website:**
    - /products/<product_id>: Display details of a specific product.
    - /cart: Display the user's shopping cart (GET), add items to the cart (POST), and update/remove items (PUT/DELETE).
- **Social Media Platform:**
    - /users/<username>: Display a user's profile.
    - /posts/<post_id>: Display a specific post.
    - /users/<username>/friends: List a user's friends.

Addressing Potential Questions:

- **"How can I handle complex URL patterns?"**
    - For more complex URL patterns, you can use regular expressions within the @app.route() decorator.
- **"What is the best practice for handling HTTP methods?"**
    - Use the appropriate HTTP method for each operation (e.g., GET for retrieving data, POST for creating data, PUT for updating data, DELETE for deleting data).
    - Always validate and sanitize user input to prevent security vulnerabilities.

- **"How can I handle errors in routing?"**
    - Use error handlers (e.g., @app.errorhandler(404)) to provide custom error pages for specific HTTP status codes.

By mastering routing and views, you'll be able to create dynamic and interactive web applications with Flask. In the following sections, we'll explore other essential aspects of Flask development, such as template rendering and database integration.

This comprehensive explanation provides a solid foundation for Computer Science students and educators. Remember to adjust the level of detail and complexity based on the specific learning objectives.

1.5 RENDERING TEMPLATES

Flask utilizes the Jinja2 templating engine to dynamically generate HTML content. This allows you to separate the presentation logic from the application logic, making your code more maintainable and easier to read.

1. Using the Jinja2 Templating Engine

- **Creating a Template:** Create an HTML file (e.g., index.html) in a directory named templates within your Flask application's root directory.
- **Rendering a Template:**

```python
from flask import Flask, render_template

app = Flask(__name__)

@app.route('/')
def index():
    return render_template('index.html')
```

- ○ render_template() [1] function loads the specified template file and renders it into a string of HTML.

2. Passing Data to Templates

- **Passing Variables:**

```python
@app.route('/')
def index():
    name = 'John Doe'
    age = 30
    return render_template('index.html', name=name, age=age)
```

- You can pass variables to the template as keyword arguments to render_template().

- **Accessing Variables in Templates:**

```html
<!DOCTYPE html>
<html>
<head>
  <title>My Web Page</title>
</head>
<body>
  <h1>Hello, {{ name }}!</h1>
  <p>You are {{ age }} years old.</p>
</body>
</html>
```

- In the template, use double curly braces {{ variable_name }} to access the variables passed from the view function.

3. Creating HTML Templates with Jinja2 Syntax

- **Variables:**
    - o Access variables as shown above: {{ variable_name }}
- **Control Flow:**
    - o **Conditional Statements:**

```
{% if age >= 18 %}
    <p>You are an adult.</p>
{% else %}
    <p>You are a minor.</p>
{% endif %}
```

    - o **Loops:**

```
<ul>
    {% for item in items %}
        <li>{{ item }}</li>
    {% endfor %}
</ul>
```

- **Filters:**
    - o Modify the output of variables:

```
<p>The current date and time is: {{ current_time.strftime('%Y-%m-%d %H:%M:%S') }}</p>
```

        - ▪ strftime() is a filter that formats the date and time.

- **Macros:**
  - o Define reusable blocks of HTML code.
- **Includes:**
  - o Include other templates within a template.

Real-World Scenarios:

- **Blog Application:**
  - o Display a list of blog posts with titles, summaries, and author information.
  - o Render individual blog posts with detailed content and comments.
- **E-commerce Website:**
  - o Display product listings with images, prices, and descriptions.
  - o Render product detail pages with more information and customer reviews.

Addressing Potential Questions:

- **"How do I debug template errors?"**
  - o Enable debug mode in your Flask application (app.run(debug=True)) to get more informative error messages.
  - o Use a debugger to step through the code and inspect variables.

- **"What are the security considerations when using templates?"**
  - ○ **Cross-Site Scripting (XSS):** Always escape user-provided data before rendering it in templates to prevent XSS attacks. Jinja2 provides autoescaping by default, but it's essential to understand how it works.
  - ○ **Template Injection:** Avoid allowing users to directly influence the template code that is rendered.
- **"Where can I find more information about Jinja2?"**
  - ○ Refer to the official Jinja2 documentation: https://jinja.palletsprojects.com/

By effectively utilizing Jinja2 templates, you can create dynamic and user-friendly web interfaces for your Flask applications. In the next section, we'll delve into working with forms, which is crucial for user input and interaction.

This explanation provides a comprehensive overview of template rendering in Flask. Remember to adjust the level of detail and complexity based on the specific learning objectives of your audience.

1.6 WORKING WITH FORMS

Forms are essential for user interaction in web applications, allowing users to input data, submit requests, and control application flow. Flask provides mechanisms to handle form submissions and validate user input.

1. Handling Form Submissions with the request Object

- **Accessing Form Data:**

from flask import Flask, request, render_template

app = Flask(__name__)

@app.route('/submit', methods=['POST'])
def submit_form():
    name = request.form['name']
    email = request.form['email']
    # Process the form data (e.g., save to database)
    return 'Form submitted successfully!'
```

* The `request.form` attribute provides access to the data submitted in the form.

* You can access individual form fields using their names (e.g., `request.form['name']`).
```

- **Handling File Uploads:**

```python
from flask import Flask, request, render_template

app = Flask(__name__)

@app.route('/upload', methods=['POST'])
def upload_file():
    file = request.files['file']
    if file:
        # Save the uploaded file to a specific location
        file.save(f'uploads/{file.filename}')
        return 'File uploaded successfully!'
    return 'No file uploaded'
```

  o The request.files attribute provides access to uploaded files.

2. Creating HTML Forms with Flask-WTF

Flask-WTF is a popular extension that simplifies form creation and validation.

- **Installation:**

```
pip install Flask-WTF
```

- **Creating a Form Class:**

```python
from flask_wtf import FlaskForm
from wtforms import StringField, SubmitField
from wtforms.validators import DataRequired
```

```
class ContactForm(FlaskForm):
    name = StringField('Name', validators=[DataRequired()])
    email = StringField('Email', validators=[DataRequired()])
    submit = SubmitField('Submit')
```

- o Define form fields using WTForms classes (e.g., StringField, TextAreaField, SelectField).
- o Add validators to enforce data constraints (e.g., DataRequired, Email).

- **Rendering the Form in a Template:**

```
<form method="POST" action="{{ url_for('contact') }}">
    {{ form.hidden_tag() }}
    {{ form.name.label }} {{ form.name() }}<br>
    {{ form.email.label }} {{ form.email() }}<br>
    {{ form.submit() }}
</form>
```

- o form.hidden_tag() generates a hidden field for CSRF protection.

- **Handling Form Submission in the View Function:**

```
from flask import Flask, render_template
from .forms import ContactForm

app = Flask(__name__)

@app.route('/contact', methods=['GET', 'POST'])
def contact():
    form = ContactForm()
```

```
if form.validate_on_submit():
    # Process the form data
    return 'Form submitted successfully!'
return render_template('contact.html', form=form)
```

- o form.validate_on_submit() checks if the form has been submitted and the data is valid.

3. Validating Form Data

- **Built-in Validators:** WTForms provides a variety of built-in validators (e.g., DataRequired, Email, Length, EqualTo).
- **Custom Validators:** Create custom validation functions to enforce specific requirements.
- **Error Handling:** Display validation errors to the user using Jinja2 templates.

Real-World Scenarios:

- **User Registration:** Validate user input (username, email, password) to ensure data integrity and prevent security issues.
- **Product Search:** Validate search queries to prevent invalid input and potential security vulnerabilities.
- **Contact Form:** Validate email addresses and other contact information to ensure data quality.

Addressing Potential Questions:

- **"How can I improve the user experience with form validation?"**
    - Provide clear and helpful error messages to guide users in correcting their input.
    - Use client-side JavaScript for initial validation to provide immediate feedback to the user.
    - Consider using AJAX to submit form data asynchronously for a smoother user experience.
- **"What are the security implications of form handling?"**
    - **Cross-Site Request Forgery (CSRF):** Implement CSRF protection measures (e.g., using Flask-WTF's csrf_token()).
    - **Input Sanitization:** Always sanitize user input to prevent security vulnerabilities like SQL injection and cross-site scripting (XSS).

By effectively handling forms, you can create user-friendly and secure web applications that provide a seamless user experience.

This comprehensive explanation provides a solid foundation for Computer Science students and educators. Remember to adjust the level of detail and complexity based on the specific learning objectives.

Note: This explanation provides a basic overview. For more in-depth information and advanced usage of Flask-WTF, refer to the official documentation: https://flask-wtf.readthedocs.io/en/latest/

1.7 STATIC FILES

Static files are assets like CSS, JavaScript, images, and other resources that remain unchanged during the application's execution. Flask provides a convenient way to serve these files directly to the browser.

1. Serving Static Files (CSS, JavaScript, Images)

- **Default Behavior:** By default, Flask expects static files to reside in a folder named static within your application's root directory.

- **Accessing Static Files in Templates:**

```html
<!DOCTYPE html>
<html>
<head>
  <title>My Web Page</title>
  <link rel="stylesheet" href="{{ url_for('static',
filename='css/style.css') }}">
</head>
<body>
  <img src="{{ url_for('static', filename='images/logo.png') }}">
</body>
</html>
```

   o The url_for('static', filename='...') function generates the correct URL for the static file.

2. Configuring Static File Paths

- **Changing the Default Path:** If you prefer a different location for your static files, you can configure it in your Flask application:

```python
from flask import Flask

app = Flask(__name__, static_folder='assets')
```

  - This example sets the static folder to assets instead of the default static.

- **Serving Files from a Different Directory:**

```python
from flask import Flask, send_from_directory

app = Flask(__name__)

@app.route('/uploads/<filename>')
def uploaded_file(filename):
    return send_from_directory(app.config['UPLOAD_FOLDER'], filename)
```

  - This example defines a custom route to serve files from a specific directory (configured in app.config['UPLOAD_FOLDER']).

Real-World Scenarios:

- **E-commerce Website:** Serving product images, CSS for styling, and JavaScript for interactive elements.
- **Social Media Platform:** Serving user profile pictures, background images, and client-side JavaScript for features like image uploads.
- **Blog Application:** Serving CSS for styling, JavaScript for dynamic features (e.g., commenting, liking), and potentially images or other media files.

Addressing Potential Questions:

- **"How can I improve the performance of static file delivery?"**
  - **Caching:** Configure browser caching headers to improve page load times by allowing browsers to cache static files for a certain period.
  - **CDN (Content Delivery Network):** Utilize a CDN to distribute static files across multiple servers, reducing latency and improving loading times for users in different locations.
- **"What are the security considerations for serving static files?"**
  - **File Uploads:** Implement proper security measures when handling file uploads to prevent malicious file uploads (e.g., executable files) and ensure that uploaded files are stored in a secure location.

31

- o **Cross-Site Scripting (XSS):** If you allow users to upload JavaScript files, carefully sanitize and validate the uploaded content to prevent XSS vulnerabilities.
- **"Can I serve static files from a different server?"**
  - o Yes, you can configure your web server (e.g., Nginx, Apache) to serve static files directly, offloading this responsibility from your Flask application. This can improve performance and scalability.

Key Considerations:

- **Organization:** Keep your static files well-organized within the static directory (or your chosen directory) for better maintainability.
- **Versioning:** Consider using a versioning system (e.g., adding a version number to file names) to facilitate caching and easily update static files.
- **Security:** Always prioritize security when handling static files, especially when dealing with user-generated content.

By effectively managing static files, you can enhance the user experience of your Flask applications by ensuring fast loading times and visually appealing presentations.

This comprehensive explanation provides a solid foundation for Computer Science students and educators. Remember to adjust the level of detail and complexity based on the specific learning objectives.

CHAPTER 2.

INTERMEDIATE FLASK

2.1 DATABASE INTEGRATION

Most real-world web applications require persistent data storage. Flask itself doesn't come with built-in database functionality, but it seamlessly integrates with various database systems.

1. Working with SQL Databases

- **Popular Choices:**
    - **SQLite:** A lightweight, file-based database ideal for smaller projects and development environments.
    - **MySQL:** A widely-used, robust, and open-source relational database system.
    - **PostgreSQL:** A powerful and feature-rich open-source database known for its advanced features and strong support for complex data types.
- **Direct Database Interactions:** You can directly interact with SQL databases using the sqlite3, mysql.connector, or psycopg2 libraries (for SQLite, MySQL, and PostgreSQL, respectively). However, this approach can lead to repetitive and error-prone code.

2. Using an Object-Relational Mapper (ORM) like SQLAlchemy

- **What is an ORM?**
  - An ORM (Object-Relational Mapper) acts as an intermediary between your Python objects and the relational database.
  - It simplifies database interactions by allowing you to work with objects instead of raw SQL queries.
- **Benefits of SQLAlchemy:**
  - **Simplified Database Interactions:** Write Python code to define database tables and interact with data, reducing the need for writing raw SQL.
  - **Improved Code Maintainability:** ORMs promote cleaner and more maintainable code by abstracting away many database-specific details.
  - **Cross-Database Compatibility:** SQLAlchemy supports a wide range of databases, making it easier to switch between different database systems.

3. Creating Database Models and Interacting with Them

- **Defining Models:**

```python

from flask_sqlalchemy import SQLAlchemy

db = SQLAlchemy()
```

```
class User(db.Model):
    id = db.Column(db.Integer, primary_key=True)
    username = db.Column(db.String(80), unique=True, nullable=False)
    email = db.Column(db.String(120), unique=True, nullable=False)
    # ... other fields ...

class Post(db.Model):
    id = db.Column(db.Integer, primary_key=True)
    title = db.Column(db.String(120), nullable=False)
    content = db.Column(db.Text)
    user_id = db.Column(db.Integer, db.ForeignKey('user.id'))
    user = db.relationship('User', backref=db.backref('posts', lazy=True))
    # ... other fields ...
```

- **Creating Database Tables:**

```
with app.app_context():
    db.create_all()
```

- **Inserting Data:**

```
new_user = User(username='john_doe',
email='john.doe@example.com')
db.session.add(new_user)
db.session.commit()
```

- **Querying Data:**

```
all_users = User.query.all()
user = User.query.filter_by(username='john_doe').first()
posts = Post.query.filter_by(user=user).all()
```

- **Updating and Deleting Data:**

```
user.username = 'updated_username'
db.session.commit()


db.session.delete(user)
db.session.commit()
```

Real-World Scenarios:

- **E-commerce:** Store product information, customer details, orders, and inventory.
- **Social Media:** Store user profiles, posts, comments, likes, and relationships between users.
- **Blog:** Store blog posts, comments, and user information.

Addressing Potential Questions:

- **"Should I always use an ORM?"**
  - For most Flask applications, using an ORM like SQLAlchemy is highly recommended. It simplifies database interactions and improves code maintainability. However, for very simple applications or when you need to execute complex SQL queries that are difficult to express with the ORM, direct database interactions might be necessary.
- **"How do I choose the right database for my project?"**
  - Consider factors such as project size, data volume, performance requirements, and features (e.g., full-text

search, spatial data support). SQLite is suitable for small projects, while MySQL and PostgreSQL are better suited for larger and more complex applications.

- **"What are some best practices for database design?"**
  - o Design your database schema carefully to ensure data integrity and efficiency.
  - o Normalize your data to reduce redundancy and improve data consistency.
  - o Consider using indexes to improve query performance.

By mastering database integration with Flask, you'll be able to build more robust and data-driven web applications. In the next section, we'll explore user authentication, a critical aspect of many web applications.

Note: This explanation provides a basic overview. For more in-depth information and advanced usage of SQLAlchemy, refer to the official documentation: https://docs.sqlalchemy.org/en/20/

This comprehensive explanation provides a solid foundation for Computer Science students and educators. Remember to adjust the level of detail and complexity based on the specific learning objectives.

2.2 USER AUTHENTICATION

User authentication is a crucial aspect of many web applications, enabling secure access to restricted areas and personalized experiences. This section explores key concepts and best practices for implementing user authentication in Flask.

1. Implementing User Registration and Login

- **Registration:**
    - Create a registration form for users to provide credentials (username/email, password).
    - Validate user input (e.g., email format, password strength).
    - Hash and salt the user's password before storing it in the database (see below).
    - Create a new user account in the database.
- **Login:**
    - Create a login form for users to enter their credentials.
    - Retrieve the user's information from the database based on their username/email.
    - Compare the provided password with the hashed password stored in the database.
    - If the credentials are valid, log the user in and redirect them to the appropriate page.

2. Password Hashing and Salting

- **Hashing:**
  - Never store passwords in plain text.
  - Use strong hashing algorithms like bcrypt or Argon2 to irreversibly transform passwords into hashes.
  - Even if the database is compromised, attackers cannot easily recover the original passwords.

- **Salting:**
  - Add a unique "salt" (random value) to each user's password before hashing it.
  - This adds an extra layer of security, making it more difficult for attackers to use pre-computed rainbow tables to crack passwords.

3. Session Management and User Authentication

- **Sessions:**
  - Flask uses sessions to maintain user state across multiple requests.
  - A session is typically stored as a cookie on the client-side and identified by a unique session ID.
  - The session ID is used to retrieve user data from the server-side.

- **Authentication:**
  - After successful login, store the user's ID (or other identifying information) in the session.

o   Use the session to determine the current user in subsequent requests.

4. Using Flask-Login or Flask-Security

- **Flask-Login:**
  - o   A lightweight extension that provides user session management and simplifies common authentication tasks.
  - o   Handles user login, logout, and session management.
  - o   Provides a @login_required decorator to protect routes.
- **Flask-Security:**
  - o   A more feature-rich extension that provides a comprehensive set of authentication and authorization features.
  - o   Includes support for features like:
    - ▪   Password recovery
    - ▪   Two-factor authentication
    - ▪   Role-based access control

Real-World Scenarios:

- **E-commerce:** User accounts for ordering, managing orders, and accessing personalized recommendations.
- **Social Media:** User accounts for creating profiles, posting content, and interacting with other users.
- **Content Management Systems (CMS):** User roles and permissions for content creators, editors, and administrators.

Addressing Potential Questions:

- **"What are the security implications of poor password handling?"**
    - Compromised user accounts, data breaches, and identity theft.
- **"How can I protect user data from unauthorized access?"**
    - Use HTTPS to encrypt communication between the client and server.
    - Implement strong password policies and enforce password complexity requirements.
    - Regularly review and update security measures.
- **"Which authentication solution is best for my project?"**
    - Flask-Login is suitable for simpler applications with basic authentication needs.
    - Flask-Security is a more robust solution for complex applications with advanced authentication and authorization requirements.

Key Considerations:

- **Security:** Always prioritize security when implementing user authentication. Follow best practices for password hashing, session management, and input validation.
- **User Experience:** Design the registration and login processes to be user-friendly and minimize friction.

41

- **Maintainability:** Choose an authentication solution that is easy to maintain and extend as your application grows.

By implementing secure and robust user authentication, you can build trust with your users and protect their sensitive information.

Note: This explanation provides a basic overview. For more in-depth information and advanced usage of Flask-Login and Flask-Security, refer to their respective documentations:

- **Flask-Login:** https://flask-login.readthedocs.io/en/latest/
- **Flask-Security:** https://flask-security.readthedocs.io/en/stable/

This comprehensive explanation provides a solid foundation for Computer Science students and educators. Remember to adjust the level of detail and complexity based on the specific learning objectives.

2.3 API DEVELOPMENT

APIs (Application Programming Interfaces) are crucial for modern web applications, enabling communication and data exchange between different systems. Flask provides an excellent foundation for building RESTful APIs, which adhere to specific architectural constraints for creating web services.

1. Building RESTful APIs with Flask

- **Core Principles:**
  - o **Resources:** Represent data as resources (e.g., users, products, orders).
  - o **HTTP Methods:** Utilize standard HTTP methods:
    - **GET:** Retrieve data (read).
    - **POST:** Create new data.
    - **PUT:** Update existing data.
    - **DELETE:** Remove data.
  - o **Status Codes:** Return appropriate HTTP status codes (e.g., 200 OK, 404 Not Found, 500 Internal Server Error) to indicate the outcome of API requests.
- **Example:**

```
from flask import Flask, jsonify

app = Flask(__name__)

@app.route('/users', methods=['GET'])
def get_users():
```

```
users = [
    {'id': 1, 'name': 'John Doe'},
    {'id': 2, 'name': 'Jane Doe'}
]
return jsonify(users)
```

2. Serializing Data with Libraries like Marshmallow

- **Data Serialization:** Converting complex data structures (like Python objects) into formats suitable for data exchange (e.g., JSON).
- **Marshmallow:** A powerful library for data serialization and deserialization. It allows you to define schemas that describe the structure of your data, making it easier to validate and transform data between Python objects and their serialized representations.

```
from flask import Flask, jsonify, request
from flask_marshmallow import Marshmallow
from flask_sqlalchemy import SQLAlchemy

ma = Marshmallow()

class UserSchema(ma.Schema):
    id = ma.Integer()
    name = ma.String()

# ... (rest of the code) ...
```

- **Benefits of Using Marshmallow:**
  - **Data Validation:** Enforce data integrity by defining validation rules within the schema.
  - **Code Reusability:** Reuse schemas for both serialization and deserialization.
  - **Improved Readability:** Schemas provide a clear and concise representation of your data structure.

3. Handling API Requests

- **GET Requests:** Retrieve data from the server.
- **POST Requests:** Create new resources on the server.
- **PUT Requests:** Update existing resources.
- **DELETE Requests:** Remove resources from the server.
- **Example:**

```python
@app.route('/users/<int:user_id>', methods=['PUT'])
def update_user(user_id):
    user = User.query.get(user_id)
    if user:
        # Update user data
        user.name = request.json.get('name')
        db.session.commit()
        return user_schema.jsonify(user)
    else:
        return jsonify({'message': 'User not found'}), 404
```

Real-World Scenarios:

- **E-commerce:** APIs for product catalogs, order management, and payment processing.
- **Social Media:** APIs for user interactions, content sharing, and third-party integrations.
- **IoT (Internet of Things):** APIs for controlling devices, collecting sensor data, and managing device configurations.

Addressing Potential Questions:

- **"What are the benefits of using RESTful APIs?"**
  - **Platform-agnostic:** APIs can be consumed by various clients (web, mobile, desktop).
  - **Flexibility:** Easily integrate with different applications and services.
  - **Scalability:** APIs can be scaled independently of the client applications.
- **"How can I document my API?"**
  - **Swagger/OpenAPI:** A popular specification for describing RESTful APIs.
  - **Documentation Tools:** Utilize tools like Swagger UI or Postman to generate interactive API documentation.
- **"What are some best practices for API design?"**
  - **Versioning:** Implement API versioning to manage changes and avoid breaking existing clients.

- Security: Implement appropriate authentication and authorization mechanisms (e.g., API keys, OAuth).
- Error Handling: Return meaningful error responses with appropriate HTTP status codes.

By mastering API development with Flask, you can create powerful and flexible applications that can interact with a wide range of services and systems.

Note: This explanation provides a basic overview. For more in-depth information and advanced usage of Flask for API development, consider exploring resources like the Flask-RESTful extension and the Flask documentation.

This comprehensive explanation provides a solid foundation for Computer Science students and educators. Remember to adjust the level of detail and complexity based on the specific learning objectives.

2.4 TESTING

Thorough testing is crucial for building robust and reliable web applications. Writing effective tests helps to:

- **Catch bugs early:** Identify and fix issues before they reach production.
- **Improve code quality:** Encourage writing more modular and maintainable code.
- **Increase confidence:** Ensure that changes to the codebase do not introduce unintended side effects.

1. Writing Unit Tests for Flask Applications

- **Unit Tests:** Focus on testing individual components of your application in isolation (e.g., individual functions, classes, or modules).
- **Key Concepts:**
  - **Test Cases:** Individual units of testing that verify specific functionality.
  - **Assertions:** Use built-in functions like assertEqual, assertTrue, assertFalse to verify expected outcomes.
  - **Test Suites:** Collections of related test cases.

2. Using Testing Frameworks

- **unittest:** Python's built-in unit testing framework. Provides a structured way to organize and run tests.

```python
import unittest
from your_app import app

class YourTestCase(unittest.TestCase):
    def setUp(self):
        self.app = app.test_client()

    def test_index(self):
        response = self.app.get('/')
        self.assertEqual(response.status_code, 200)
        self.assertIn(b'Hello, World!', response.data)
```

- **pytest:** A more modern and flexible testing framework. Offers features like fixtures, parametrization, and plugins for enhanced testing capabilities.

```python
from your_app import app

def test_index():
    with app.test_client() as client:
        response = client.get('/')
        assert response.status_code == 200
        assert b'Hello, World!' in response.data
```

3. Testing Routes, Views, and Database Interactions

- **Testing Routes:**
  - ○ Verify that routes return the expected HTTP status codes (e.g., 200 OK, 404 Not Found).
  - ○ Check that routes return the correct data (e.g., JSON responses, HTML templates).
  - ○ Test different HTTP methods (GET, POST, PUT, DELETE).

- **Testing Views:**
  - ○ Test the logic within your view functions, including data processing, database interactions, and template rendering.
  - ○ Use mock objects to simulate dependencies (e.g., database connections) and isolate the behavior of your view functions.

- **Testing Database Interactions:**
  - ○ Test database operations like creating, reading, updating, and deleting records.
  - ○ Use a testing database to avoid interfering with your production data.
  - ○ Test for data integrity and consistency.

Real-World Scenarios:

- **E-commerce:** Test product catalog, order processing, and payment gateways.
- **Social Media:** Test user registration, login, posting, and user interactions.
- **API:** Test API endpoints for different HTTP methods, data validation, and error handling.

Addressing Potential Questions:

- **"How do I write effective unit tests?"**
  - Keep tests small and focused.
  - Use clear and concise assertions.
  - Test edge cases and boundary conditions.
  - Write tests early and often.
- **"What are the benefits of using a testing framework like pytest?"**
  - **Improved readability:** Pytest's syntax is more concise and easier to read.
  - **Enhanced features:** Fixtures, parametrization, and plugins provide powerful testing capabilities.
  - **Large community and ecosystem:** Extensive documentation and a wide range of plugins available.
- **"How do I test database interactions effectively?"**
  - **Use a testing database:** Avoid modifying your production data.
  - **Use fixtures to set up and tear down test data.**

o   **Test different scenarios:** Successful operations, invalid input, and error handling.

By writing comprehensive tests for your Flask applications, you can significantly improve their quality, reliability, and maintainability.

Note: This explanation provides a basic overview. For more in-depth information and advanced testing techniques, refer to the documentation for unittest and pytest, as well as resources specifically focused on testing Flask applications.

This comprehensive explanation provides a solid foundation for Computer Science students and educators. Remember to adjust the level of detail and complexity based on the specific learning objectives.

CHAPTER 3.

ADVANCED FLASK

3.1 DEPLOYMENT

Deploying a Flask application to production involves making it accessible to the public on a live server. This section covers key aspects of the deployment process.

1. Deploying Flask Applications to Production Servers

- **Popular Platforms:**
  - **Cloud Platforms:** Heroku, AWS (Amazon Web Services), Google Cloud Platform, Azure, DigitalOcean. These platforms offer various services like compute instances, databases, and load balancing, making it easier to deploy and scale applications.
  - **Containerization:** Deploying your application as a Docker container provides portability and ensures consistent behavior across different environments.

- **Deployment Strategies:**
  - **Manual Deployment:** Upload your application files to the server manually (e.g., using SSH or FTP).
  - **Continuous Integration/Continuous Deployment (CI/CD):** Automate the deployment process using tools like Jenkins, GitLab CI/CD, or GitHub Actions. This ensures that code changes are automatically built, tested, and deployed to production.

2. Setting Up a WSGI Server

- **WSGI (Web Server Gateway Interface):** A standard interface between a web server (like Apache or Nginx) and a Python web application (like Flask).
- **Popular WSGI Servers:**
  - **Gunicorn:** A pre-fork worker model server known for its performance and scalability.
  - **uWSGI:** A versatile and highly configurable WSGI server with support for multiple protocols and features.
  - **Waitress:** A production-ready WSGI server that is easy to use and suitable for smaller applications.

- **Example Gunicorn Command:**

```
gunicorn --workers 4 --bind 0.0.0.0:8000 your_app:app
```

  - --workers 4: Specifies the number of worker processes to handle requests concurrently.
  - --bind 0.0.0.0:8000: Specifies the host and port for the server to listen on.

3. Configuring for Production Environments

- **Environment Variables:** Store sensitive information (e.g., database credentials, API keys) as environment variables. This helps to keep your code secure and makes it easier to manage different environments (development, staging, production).
- **Caching:** Implement caching mechanisms (e.g., using libraries like flask-caching) to improve performance by storing frequently accessed data in memory.
- **Logging:** Configure robust logging to monitor application behavior, identify errors, and troubleshoot issues.
- **Security:** Implement security measures like HTTPS (SSL/TLS), input validation, and protection against common web vulnerabilities (e.g., SQL injection, cross-site scripting).

Real-World Scenarios:

- Deploying an e-commerce application to AWS EC2 instances.
- Deploying a social media platform using Docker and Kubernetes on Google Cloud.
- **Deploying a RESTful API to Heroku for easy scaling and management.

Addressing Potential Questions:

- **"What factors should I consider when choosing a deployment platform?"**
  - **Scalability and performance requirements:** Can the platform handle the expected traffic and data volume?
  - **Cost:** Evaluate the pricing models of different platforms and choose the most cost-effective option for your needs.
  - **Ease of use:** Consider the ease of deployment, management, and scaling on the chosen platform.
  - **Support:** Evaluate the level of support and documentation provided by the platform.
- **"How can I ensure the security of my deployed application?"**
  - **Regular security audits:** Conduct regular security assessments to identify and address vulnerabilities.

- o **Keep software updated:** Regularly update your application and dependencies to patch security vulnerabilities.

- o **Implement proper access controls:** Restrict access to your production servers and databases.

- **"What are some best practices for production deployments?"**

  - o **Use a version control system (e.g., Git):** Track all code changes and facilitate rollbacks if necessary.

  - o **Implement a CI/CD pipeline:** Automate the deployment process to reduce errors and improve efficiency.

  - o **Monitor application performance:** Use monitoring tools to track key metrics (e.g., request latency, error rates) and identify potential issues.

By carefully planning and executing the deployment process, you can ensure that your Flask applications are stable, scalable, and secure in production environments.

Note: This explanation provides a basic overview. For more in-depth information and specific deployment guides for different platforms, refer to the documentation for those platforms and explore resources like the Flask documentation.

3.2 ADVANCED TEMPLATING

Jinja2, the templating engine at the heart of Flask, offers a rich set of features beyond basic variable substitution. Mastering these advanced techniques enhances code reusability, improves maintainability, and enables more complex and dynamic web pages.

1. Custom Filters and Tests

- **Filters:** Modify the output of variables within templates.
    - **Example:**

    ```
    {{ some_text | capitalize }}
    {{ some_number | round(2) }}
    ```

    - **Creating Custom Filters:**

    ```
    from jinja2 import Environment

    env = Environment()

    @env.filter
    def my_filter(value):
        # Your custom logic here
        return modified_value
    ```

- **Tests:** Check if a variable meets certain conditions.
  - o **Example:**

```
{% if some_value is defined %}
    <p>The value is defined.</p>
{% endif %}
```

  - o **Creating Custom Tests:**

```
@env.test
def my_test(value):
    # Your custom logic here
    return True or False
```

2. Macros and Includes for Code Reusability

- **Macros:** Define reusable blocks of HTML code within a template.
  - o **Example:**

```
{% macro render_item(item) %}
    <div class="item">
        {{ item.name }}
    </div>
{% endmacro %}

{% for item in items %}
    {{ render_item(item) }}
{% endfor %}
```

- **Includes:** Include other templates within a template.
  - **Example:**

```
{% include 'header.html' %}
<div class="content">

  ...

</div>
{% include 'footer.html' %}
```

3. Advanced Templating Techniques

- **Template Inheritance:** Create a base template with common elements (e.g., header, footer, navigation) and extend it in other templates to inherit those elements. This promotes code reusability and consistency across your application.
- **Context Processors:** Functions that add global variables to the template context, making them available in all templates.
- **Sandboxing:** Restrict the capabilities of the Jinja2 environment to prevent potential security vulnerabilities.

Real-World Scenarios

- **E-commerce Website:**
  - Create a reusable macro for displaying product cards.
  - Use template inheritance to create a consistent layout for all product pages.
  - Implement custom filters for formatting prices and applying discounts.

- **Blog Application:**
  - o Create a macro for displaying blog post excerpts.
  - o Use template inheritance to create a consistent layout for all blog posts.
  - o Implement custom filters for formatting dates and highlighting keywords.

Addressing Potential Questions:

- **"How can I avoid over-engineering templates?"**
  - o Use advanced features judiciously. Keep templates focused on presentation and avoid embedding complex logic within them.
- **"How can I ensure the security of my templates?"**
  - o **Autoescaping:** Jinja2 automatically escapes HTML by default, but it's essential to understand how it works and handle user-provided content carefully.
  - o **Sandboxing:** Restrict the capabilities of the Jinja2 environment to prevent potential security vulnerabilities.
- **"Where can I find more advanced Jinja2 examples and best practices?"**
  - o Refer to the official Jinja2 documentation: https://jinja.palletsprojects.com/
  - o Explore online resources and tutorials for advanced Jinja2 usage.

By mastering these advanced templating techniques, you can create more sophisticated, maintainable, and visually appealing web interfaces for your Flask applications.

This comprehensive explanation provides a solid foundation for Computer Science students and educators. Remember to adjust the level of detail and complexity based on the specific learning objectives.

3.3 SECURITY BEST PRACTICES

Security is paramount in web application development. Neglecting security measures can lead to serious consequences, such as data breaches, financial losses, and reputational damage. This section focuses on critical security best practices for Flask applications.

1. Preventing Common Web Vulnerabilities

- **Cross-Site Scripting (XSS):**
  - **Description:** Attacks that inject malicious scripts into web pages viewed by other users.
  - **Prevention:**
    - **Input Sanitization:** Escape or encode user-supplied data before rendering it in templates or displaying it in responses.
      - Use Jinja2's autoescaping feature and the escape() function.
    - **Output Encoding:** Ensure proper encoding of output to prevent unexpected interpretations by the browser.
    - **Content Security Policy (CSP):** A browser mechanism that restricts the sources from which content (like scripts) can be loaded.
- **Cross-Site Request Forgery (CSRF):**
  - **Description:** Attacks that trick users into performing actions on a website they don't intend to.

- Prevention:
  - **CSRF Tokens:** Include a unique, unpredictable token in forms and verify it on the server-side before processing the form data.
  - **Use Flask-WTF's csrf_token() for easy CSRF protection.**
- **SQL Injection:**
  - **Description:** Attacks that exploit vulnerabilities in database queries to execute unauthorized commands.
  - **Prevention:**
    - **Parameterization:** Use parameterized queries with libraries like SQLAlchemy to prevent direct SQL string concatenation.
    - **Input Validation:** Validate and sanitize all user-supplied data before using it in database queries.

2. Input Validation and Sanitization

- **Validation:** Check user input against predefined rules (e.g., data types, length, format) to ensure data integrity and prevent invalid or malicious input.
- **Sanitization:** Clean and transform user input to remove or neutralize potentially harmful characters (e.g., HTML tags, special characters).

- **Example:**

```
from werkzeug.utils import escape

@app.route('/profile', methods=['POST'])
def update_profile():
    username = request.form.get('username')
    # Sanitize username
    sanitized_username = escape(username)
    # ... further processing ...
```

3. Secure Session Management

- **HTTPS:** Always use HTTPS (HTTPS) to encrypt communication between the client and server, protecting sensitive data like session cookies.
- **Secure Cookies:**
  - o **HttpOnly flag:** Prevent JavaScript from accessing cookies, making them less vulnerable to XSS attacks.
  - o **Secure flag:** Ensure cookies are only sent over HTTPS connections.
  - o **Short session expiration:** Set appropriate session expiration times to minimize the impact of potential session hijacking.
- **Regular Session Rotation:** Invalidate and regenerate session IDs periodically to reduce the risk of session hijacking.

Real-World Scenarios:

- **E-commerce Website:** Prevent SQL injection attacks in product search queries, sanitize user-provided product descriptions, and implement CSRF protection for order processing.
- **Social Media Platform:** Prevent XSS attacks in user-generated content (e.g., posts, comments), implement secure password storage, and protect user accounts from unauthorized access.
- **Content Management System:** Implement robust input validation and sanitization for user-generated content (e.g., blog posts, images) to prevent XSS and other attacks.

Addressing Potential Questions:

- **"How can I learn more about common web vulnerabilities?"**
    - **OWASP (Open Web Application Security Project):** A valuable resource for information on web security vulnerabilities and best practices (https://owasp.org/).
    - **OWASP Cheat Sheet Series:** Provides concise and actionable guidance on various web security topics.
- **"How can I test my application for security vulnerabilities?"**
    - **Security audits:** Conduct regular security audits using automated tools and manual penetration testing.

- o Use security testing frameworks like **OWASP ZAP.**
- **"What is the role of security in the entire software development lifecycle?"**
  - o **Security should be considered throughout the entire development process:**
    - **Design phase:** Incorporate security considerations into the application architecture.
    - **Development phase:** Write secure code and perform regular code reviews.
    - **Testing phase:** Conduct thorough security testing.
    - **Deployment phase:** Deploy applications securely and monitor for vulnerabilities.

By diligently implementing these security best practices, you can significantly enhance the security and resilience of your Flask applications.

Note: This explanation provides a basic overview. For more in-depth information and advanced security techniques, refer to the OWASP resources and consult with security experts.

3.4 SCALING AND PERFORMANCE

As your Flask application grows in popularity and user base, it's crucial to ensure it can handle increasing traffic and maintain high performance. This section explores key strategies for scaling and optimizing your Flask applications.

1. Caching Mechanisms

- **Caching:** Storing frequently accessed data in memory to reduce the need to repeatedly fetch it from slower sources like databases or external APIs.
- **Popular Caching Solutions:**
    - **Memcached:** A high-performance, distributed memory object caching system.
    - **Redis:** An in-memory data store that supports various data structures (strings, hashes, lists, sets) beyond simple key-value storage.
- **Flask-Caching:** A Flask extension that provides an easy way to integrate caching into your application.
- **Example:**

```
from flask import Flask
from flask_caching import Cache

app = Flask(__name__)
cache = Cache(app, config={'CACHE_TYPE': 'simple'})

@app.route('/')
```

```
@cache.cached(timeout=60)
def index():
    # Expensive operation (e.g., database query)
    result = get_expensive_data()
    return render_template('index.html', result=result)
```

2. Asynchronous Programming with asyncio

- **Asynchronous Programming:** Enables concurrent execution of multiple tasks without blocking the main thread. This is crucial for handling I/O-bound operations (like network requests) efficiently.
- **asyncio:** Python's built-in library for asynchronous programming.
- **Example:**

```
import asyncio
from aiohttp import ClientSession

async def fetch_data(session, url):
    async with session.get(url) as response:
        return await response.json()

async def main():
    async with ClientSession() as session:
        data1 = await fetch_data(session, 'https://api1.com')
        data2 = await fetch_data(session, 'https://api2.com')
        # ... process data ...

asyncio.run(main())
```

- **Note:** While asyncio can improve performance, it introduces complexity. Carefully evaluate if it's necessary for your specific application.

3. Load Balancing and Scaling Techniques

- **Load Balancing:** Distributes incoming traffic across multiple server instances to prevent overload on a single server.
  - o **Hardware Load Balancers:** Dedicated devices or appliances that handle traffic distribution.
  - o **Software Load Balancers:** Load balancing software running on servers (e.g., Nginx, HAProxy).
- **Scaling Techniques:**
  - o **Vertical Scaling:** Increase the resources (CPU, RAM) of existing servers.
  - o **Horizontal Scaling:** Add more server instances to handle the increased load.
- **Cloud Platforms:** Leverage cloud platforms like AWS, Google Cloud, and Azure, which offer scalable infrastructure and managed services for load balancing and auto-scaling.

Real-World Scenarios:

- **E-commerce Website:** Cache product catalogs, user profiles, and frequently accessed data to improve page load times during peak traffic.

- **Social Media Platform:** Use asynchronous tasks to process user uploads, notifications, and background jobs without blocking user requests.

- **API Server:** Implement load balancing to distribute requests across multiple API server instances to handle high traffic volumes.

Addressing Potential Questions:

- **"When should I consider using caching?"**
  - When you have frequently accessed data that is relatively static or changes infrequently.
  - When you want to reduce the load on your database or external services.

- **"What are the challenges of asynchronous programming?"**
  - Debugging asynchronous code can be more challenging than synchronous code.
  - Careful consideration is needed to handle concurrency and avoid race conditions.

- **"How do I choose the right scaling strategy?"**
  - **Start with vertical scaling:** Increase resources on your existing server(s) if possible.

71

- o **Consider horizontal scaling:** Add more servers as needed to handle growing traffic.
- o **Utilize cloud platforms:** Leverage their scalability and managed services to simplify scaling operations.

By effectively implementing caching, utilizing asynchronous programming techniques, and employing appropriate scaling strategies, you can ensure that your Flask applications can handle high traffic loads, maintain responsiveness, and deliver a positive user experience.

Note: This explanation provides a basic overview. For more in-depth information and advanced scaling techniques, refer to the documentation for caching libraries (e.g., Memcached, Redis), the asyncio library, and the chosen load balancing and cloud platform.

CHAPTER 4.

REAL-WORLD PROJECTS

Building real-world projects is crucial for solidifying your understanding of Flask and gaining practical experience. Here are a few project ideas to get you started:

4.1 BUILDING A BLOG APPLICATION

- **Core Features:**
    - o   User registration and login
    - o   Create, read, update, and delete blog posts
    - o   User profiles and avatars
    - o   Commenting system
    - o   Search functionality
    - o   RSS/Atom feeds
- **Advanced Features:**
    - o   Markdown support for rich text formatting
    - o   Tagging and categorization of posts
    - o   Image and video uploads
    - o   Social media integration
- **Learning Objectives:**
    - o   Database interactions (e.g., SQLAlchemy)
    - o   User authentication and authorization
    - o   Data modeling and relationships (users, posts, comments)

- Template rendering and Jinja2 templating techniques
- File uploads and handling

4.2 CREATING A TO-DO LIST APPLICATION

- **Core Features:**
  - o Create, read, update, and delete to-do items
  - o Assign priorities and due dates to tasks
  - o Mark tasks as completed
  - o Organize tasks into lists or projects
  - o User authentication and authorization

- **Advanced Features:**
  - o Recurring tasks
  - o Reminders and notifications
  - o Collaboration features (e.g., sharing lists with others)
  - o Integration with calendar applications

- **Learning Objectives:**
  - o Database interactions (e.g., SQLite)
  - o User authentication (if applicable)
  - o Form handling and data validation
  - o JavaScript integration for interactive features

4.3 DEVELOPING A SIMPLE E-COMMERCE APPLICATION

- **Core Features:**
    - o Product catalog (displaying product information, images, prices)
    - o Shopping cart functionality
    - o User registration and order placement
    - o Payment processing integration (e.g., using a payment gateway like Stripe)
- **Advanced Features:**
    - o Inventory management
    - o Order tracking
    - o Customer reviews and ratings
    - o Recommendations and personalized offers
- **Learning Objectives:**
    - o Database interactions (e.g., for products, orders, users)
    - o User authentication and authorization
    - o Handling payments and transactions
    - o Session management for maintaining cart contents

4.4 BUILDING A SOCIAL NETWORKING PLATFORM (BASIC FUNCTIONALITY)

- **Core Features:**
  - o User registration and login
  - o User profiles with basic information
  - o Posting text updates or images
  - o Following other users
  - o Basic user feeds (displaying posts from followed users)

- **Advanced Features:**
  - o Direct messaging
  - o Notifications
  - o Groups and communities
  - o Search functionality
  - o Image and video uploads

- **Learning Objectives:**
  - o User authentication and authorization
  - o Database interactions for user profiles, posts, and relationships
  - o Handling user interactions (following, liking, commenting)
  - o Building a user-friendly interface

KEY CONSIDERATIONS FOR ALL PROJECTS:

- **Start with a Minimal Viable Product (MVP):** Focus on implementing core features first and gradually add more advanced functionality.
- **Break Down the Project:** Divide the project into smaller, more manageable tasks.
- **Test Thoroughly:** Write unit tests to ensure the correctness and reliability of your code.
- **Use Version Control:** Use Git to track changes to your code and collaborate with others.
- **Document Your Work:** Write clear and concise documentation to explain the project's architecture and how it works.

Addressing Potential Questions:

- **"How do I choose a project that's right for me?"**
  - Select a project that interests you and aligns with your learning goals.
  - Consider your current skill level and choose a project that provides a good balance of challenge and learning.
- **"Where can I find resources and inspiration for project ideas?"**
  - Explore online resources like GitHub, Codecademy, and FreeCodeCamp for project ideas and tutorials.
  - Look at existing web applications and try to recreate some of their core features.
- **"How can I overcome challenges during the project?"**

- o **Break down problems:** Divide complex tasks into smaller, more manageable steps.
- o **Consult documentation and online resources:** Refer to the Flask documentation, tutorials, and online communities for help.
- o **Debug effectively:** Use debugging tools and techniques to identify and fix issues in your code.
- o **Don't be afraid to ask for help:** Seek assistance from online communities, mentors, or fellow learners.

Building real-world projects is an essential part of the learning process. By working on these projects, you'll gain valuable practical experience, solidify your understanding of Flask concepts, and build a strong foundation for future web development endeavors.

Note: This explanation provides a basic overview. Remember to adjust the scope and complexity of these projects based on your current skill level and learning goals.

This comprehensive explanation provides a solid foundation for Computer Science students and educators. Remember to adjust the level of detail and complexity based on the specific learning objectives.

Key Considerations

Building real-world projects is not just about writing code; it's about the entire learning process. Here's a deeper dive into the key considerations:

1. Consistent Practice: The Most Important Aspect

- **"Practice Makes Perfect":** This adage holds true for Flask development. Consistent practice is essential for solidifying your understanding of concepts and building muscle memory for common tasks.
- **Small, Frequent Projects:** Instead of focusing on one massive project, start with smaller, more manageable projects. This allows you to:
    - **Focus on specific concepts:** Each project can target a particular aspect of Flask (e.g., database integration, user authentication, API development).
    - **Receive faster feedback:** Smaller projects allow for quicker iterations and easier debugging.
    - **Maintain motivation:** Completing smaller projects provides a sense of accomplishment and encourages continued learning.
- **Project Ideas:** Explore online resources like:
    - **GitHub:** Browse through open-source Flask projects for inspiration and learning opportunities.
    - **Codewars, HackerRank, LeetCode:** These platforms offer coding challenges, including many that can be adapted to Flask projects.

- Online tutorials and courses: Many platforms (e.g., Codecademy, Udemy, Coursera) offer Flask projects as part of their learning paths.

2. Utilize Online Resources

- **Flask Documentation:** The official Flask documentation is an invaluable resource: https://flask.palletsprojects.com/
- **Tutorials:**
  - **Flask Mega-Tutorial:** A comprehensive and well-regarded tutorial by Miguel Grinberg: [invalid URL removed]
  - **Codecademy, FreeCodeCamp:** Offer interactive Flask tutorials for beginners and more advanced learners.
- **Community Forums:**
  - **Stack Overflow:** A vast resource for finding answers to your Flask-related questions and learning from the experiences of others.
  - **Reddit's r/flask:** An active community forum for discussing Flask development, sharing projects, and seeking help.

3. Community Engagement

- **Learning from Others:**
  - **Open-source contributions:** Contribute to open-source Flask projects to learn from experienced developers and gain practical experience.
  - **Code reviews:** Participate in code reviews to learn from others' code and improve your own coding style.

- **Sharing Knowledge:**
  - o **Create tutorials or blog posts:** Share your learning experiences and help others in the Flask community.
  - o **Mentoring:** Offer guidance and support to other developers who are learning Flask.

4. Continuous Learning

- **Stay Updated:** The web development landscape is constantly evolving. Stay updated with the latest trends and technologies:
  - o **New Flask features:** Follow the Flask project releases and updates to learn about new features and improvements.
  - o **Emerging technologies:** Explore technologies like WebSockets, GraphQL, and serverless computing, and how they can be integrated with Flask.
  - o **Security best practices:** Stay informed about the latest security vulnerabilities and best practices for building secure web applications.

Addressing Potential Questions:

- **"How do I overcome the feeling of being stuck?"**
  - o **Break down the problem:** Divide the problem into smaller, more manageable subproblems.
  - o **Debug systematically:** Use debugging tools and techniques to identify and fix errors.
  - o **Consult online resources and seek help:** Refer to the Flask documentation, search for solutions online, and ask for help from the community.
- **"How do I stay motivated during the learning process?"**

- o **Set realistic goals:** Break down your learning journey into smaller, achievable milestones.
- o **Celebrate your accomplishments:** Acknowledge and reward your progress to stay motivated.
- o **Find a learning buddy:** Collaborate with others who are learning Flask to stay motivated and share your progress.

- **"How do I know if I'm learning effectively?"**
  - o **Reflect on your learning:** Regularly assess your progress and identify areas for improvement.
  - o **Build real-world projects:** Apply your knowledge to practical projects and see the results firsthand.
  - o **Teach others:** Explain concepts to others to solidify your own understanding.

By consistently practicing, utilizing available resources, actively engaging with the community, and embracing continuous learning, you can build a strong foundation in Flask development and become a proficient web developer.

This page is intentionally left blank.

ABOUT THE AUTHOR

Mark John Lado is an accomplished Information System Specialist with a strong background in education and technology. He holds a Master's degree in Information Technology from Northern Negros State College of Science and Technology and is currently pursuing his Doctorate in the same field.

Mark boasts a diverse professional experience, having served as an ICT Instructor/Coordinator at Carmen Christian School Inc., a Part-time Information Technology Instructor at the University of the Visayas, and a Faculty member at Colegio de San Antonio de Padua and Cebu Technological University. He is currently a Faculty member at the College of Technology and Engineering at Cebu Technological University.

His expertise extends beyond the classroom, encompassing Object-Oriented Programming, Teacher Mentoring, Computer Hardware, Software System Analysis, and Web Development. He actively participates in the Philippine Society of Information Technology Educators (PSITE) as a member and has contributed to the academic community through the publication of his research article, "A Wireless Digital Public Address with Voice Alarm and Text-to-speech Feature for Different Campuses," in Globus An International Journal of Management & IT.

Mark's dedication to education and passion for technology are evident in his contributions to various educational institutions, including Cebu

Technological University, University of the Visayas - Danao Campus, Colegio de San Antonio de Padua, and Carmen Christian School Inc.

Biography Source:

https://www.biographies.net/

Authors' Official Website:

https://markjohnlado.com/

This page is intentionally left blank.